Gary Jones

Amsterdam

This book was professionally typeset on Reedsy.
Find out more at reedsy.com

Contents

1

Introduction

Thank you for downloading my book.This book focuses on the Short Stay Traveler.If your time is limited in this wonderful city, then this book is perfect for you.I have put together the best Amsterdam has to offer in 3 to 4 days.

Amsterdam has a long, rich history behind it. It rose from simple beginnings and has become one of the best-planned cities of the modern world. It became the economic center of an entire nation at one time in the 17th century. And yet it owes its existence from a few simple fishing folk who just wanted to live a carefree life that has very little trouble.

Amsterdam is one of those special cities in the world that everyone knows about.It's usually one of the first recommendations of places to visit when someone travel to Europe.The reason is simple, Amsterdam is one of the most interesting places on this beautiful planet.

Amsterdam is an amazing mix of beautiful, old, new, interesting,unique,edgy,mysterious,cutting edge, modern and at times, strange.This fantastic mix of qualities creates one of the leading cities in Europe with a very interesting history.

Have a great time in Amsterdam!!

2

Amsterdam's Early Beginnings

The beginnings of Amsterdam

The beginnings of Amsterdam can be traced all the way to the 12th century. From the years 1150 to 1300, the locals who settled in the area took every effort to build dams. The idea was to contain the waters of the IJ River. The area to be covered ranged from Haarlem all the way to Zuiderzee. During this time, a small community of fishing folk began to form on the banks of the river Amstel.

They were also able to build a bridge that connected to a huge saltwater inlet where they can fish for herring among other things. The dams mainly protected the small fishing community from regular rise of the river IJ. If not then the community will get flooded every time the tide goes up.

The settlement itself was perfectly established especially for trade. The mouth of the Amstel River basically formed a rather natural harbor. Small trading ships that can travel deeper inland made their way easily into this harbor. Larger Koggeships came with their huge supply of goods to exchange and barter, bringing with them much-needed items.

Recent archaeological digs confirm that there were other people who settled in the rich area of the Amstel long before the fishing village was established. Archaeologists found pottery, pole axes, and other artifacts that dated all the way back to the New Stone Age. This means that human beings and other communities may have come and gone in the area since around 2600 BCE.

From the 12th century on, early Amsterdam increasingly became a center of trade. The beer trade strengthened commerce coming in and out of the city. Trade ties with other cities and territories in the Baltic Sea and the Hanseatic League were formed. And, during the 15th century, Amsterdam eventually became the central granary of sorts. Grains that were to be traded or transported to what was then known as the low countries of the north came from Amsterdam. The city quickly became the most important trading city in all of Holland.

Historical Trivia
Revolution and Independence

There were many reasons why the Dutch revolted against Spain. One reason, of course, was religious intolerance. Another reason was political since there was very little power granted to the local nobility. The rebellion began in 1578, and it came to be known as the Eighty Years' War. The revolt of the people eventually led to Dutch independence.

Amsterdam along with the other Dutch cities became quite tolerant. People believed whatever they wanted as long as it is within certain limits. Many sought refuge in the Dutch Republic while religious wars raged throughout Europe at the time. This paradigm of tolerance and acceptance remains today an important hallmark of Amsterdam.

The Golden Age and Modernization

The years following the Dutch independence were known as the Golden Age. Amsterdam back then gave the largest amounts of taxes compared to the other states in the country. Trade and commerce was on the rise and city's population reached its peak at 200,000.

The government was able to provide well for their constituents. A lot of essential care was provided in the form of hospitals, almshouses, churches, as well as houses for the elderly.

Eventually, the city went into a decline. The city was ravaged by the Bubonic Plague from 1663 to 1666, which should be expected from a trading hub. More than 10% of the city's population died. A lot of the rich folks closed their shops and businesses and left. The many wars of the Dutch Republic with other countries also ushered in the city's decline. World Wars I and II also contributed largely to the losses in Amsterdam.

The Jewish community was deported, which included Anne Frank. Along with their leaving was the demise of the city's diamond trade. All of the investors in the prestigious Amsterdam diamond industry were Jews.

The years 1940 to the present represented the years of recovery. The city's economy switched from industrial to that of a service economy. Economic recessions have come and gone. The city today has become one of the popular tourist destinations in the world.

3

Transport

Transport Options

Amsterdam is one of the most visited cities in Europe. That means there are a lot of transport options to get into the city. You can actually get to it by land, sea, and air. There are also a lot of cheap flights from Europe, which should be your number one option. The Schiphol Airport in Amsterdam is one of the largest and busiest airports in the world. It's the fourth largest airport in all of Europe.

Schiphol Airport Website

http://www.schiphol.nl/index_en.html

Schiphol Airport Map
https://goo.gl/maps/T1qTA7VE8dL2

Getting Around the City

Once you're in Amsterdam, there are a lot of different ways to get around from one point of interest to the other. The following are many different means of transport that you can use to get to the places you want to visit. Note that some means of transport will cost more than others.

Riding on a Bike

If you really want to travel like the Dutch people do then you better hop on a bicycle. Cycling is a way of life for the locals and this is one of the best ways to immerse yourself in the local culture. There are bike paths all over Amsterdam so don't worry about sharing the road with cars, trucks, buses, and all the other vehicles that ply the streets. There are lots of bicycle rental companies in the city and they usually charge a rental fee of eight euros.

Bike Rental Map

https://goo.gl/maps/4qViNiYzZFn

City Taxis

Taxis are more expensive than other means of transport in Amsterdam. Taxi rates begin at €1.80 per kilometer and there is also a 5 to 10 percent tip (optional). Convenience definitely comes with a price. You'll find most taxis within the tourist hubs and their service is prompt. However, note that getting one during the weekends will be a bit difficult.

Bike Taxis

So there are regular taxis and there are bicycles – the most common travel options in town; but now you can also hop on bike taxis – a combination of bicycles and taxis. It's like a gondola that's been given a modern twist. You can call it the environmentally friendly revolution.

The downside is that these things can only take two passengers at a time. It doesn't pollute the air and it doesn't make any loud noises. It squeaks from time to time and the driver has to ring the bell from time to time. These three-wheeled pedal powered taxis also come with batteries – adds extra power in case the driver takes an extra heavy passenger or when the road takes on an extra high slope. You pay 1 euro for every 3 minutes of the ride.

Trams, Trains, and Buses

Trams are considered as the best ways to go around the city. Trams will be rolling around until 12:15 am. Another option is the Amsterdam Metro System. All trips start at the Central Station. Trains are the more convenient way to travel in case you're leaving Amsterdam. If you want to reach many of the suburbs then hop on a bus. Night buses are also your option when trams have stopped running. Night bus trips start at 12:30 am and end at 7 in the morning.

Transport Website

http://en.gvb.nl/

Rent a Car

Renting a car in Amsterdam and driving in the city is not recommended for tourists. The roads can be pretty difficult to maneuver and finding a place to park will be quite a hassle. But if you insist on driving, then you can find car rentals right at the airport and in the city center.

4

Hotels

Amsterdam can be expensive, but I have made a short list of budget hotels that might be a good fit for you:

Citizenm Hotel

This lovely boutique hotel is modern with fantastic service.What makes this hotel even better is the affordable prices.This is a very good deal for a budget traveler who want to stay in a nice hotel with modern features and a nice location away from the city noise.

Phone:+31(0)208117080

citizenM Amsterdam

Prinses Irenestraat 30

1077 WX Amsterdam

Citizenm Hotel Website

https://www.citizenm.com/destinations/amsterdam/amsterdam-hotel

Citizenm Hotel Map

https://goo.gl/maps/cqCiGWBFueL2

Hotel Brouwer

If you want to stay in the center of Amsterdam and be walking distance from most things in Amsterdam, then get a room at the Hotel Brouwer.The hotel is located next to a canal and is one of the best locations in Amsterdam.

Phone:31-(0)20-624-6358

Singel 83

1012 VE Amsterdam

Hotel Brouwer Website

http://www.hotelbrouwer.nl/hoteleng.html

Hotel Brouwer Map

https://goo.gl/maps/KLMYNCFeib32

Between Art and Kitsch b&b Amsterdam

In true Amsterdam style, this hotel is something different than your normal bed and breakfast hotel.It's difficult to describe this hotel, except to say that its a mix of old, new and eccentric.If you are looking for something different then this for you.

Phone:+31 20 6790485

Ruysdaelkade 75-2

1072 AL Amsterdam

Between Art and Kitsch b&b Website
http://www.between-art-and-kitsch.com/en
Between Art and Kitsch b&b Map
https://goo.gl/maps/Vc7eDtHGhLx

Seven Bridges Hotel

The Seven Bridges is a 300-year-old hotel located in the heart of Amsterdam. The name says seven bridges, and that is what you get. The hotel has a view over seven bridges on the canal and is a classic place to stay for your short stay.

Phone: + 31-20-6231329

Seven Bridges Hotel

Reguliersgracht 31

1017 LK Amsterdam

Seven Bridges Hotel Website

http://www.sevenbridgeshotel.nl/cms/

Seven Bridges Hotel Map

https://goo.gl/maps/iDpcUykKuuA2

5

Amsterdam's Best Museums

There are a lot of reasons why Amsterdam is named as the world's 2nd best city to live in. Other than its rich history, the place also has a lot of interesting attractions. Included in this huge list of attractions is a plethora of museums. Statistics show that the city of Amsterdam has more museums than any other city in the world per square meter. That includes a lot of historical buildings that house many cultural treasures, artifacts, and art.

The following is a list of some of the most popular and important museums in Amsterdam. The list also includes a few interesting museums that don't get noticed as much as the more prominent ones.

Rijksmuseum

Rijksmuseum is the most popular museum in the city. It's actually the most popular museum in the Netherlands – well, they won't call it the Dutch national museum for nothing. It had a really huge facelift beginning in 2003. The renovation and modernization work took about ten years to complete. It was reopened to the public in April 13, 2013. The Rijksmuseum showcases the best in Dutch art. It houses some of the most important historical artifacts in the country. It also has an extensive collection of Asian and European art.

Rijksmuseum is located at Museumstraat 1, the Museum Quarter. The place is open from 9 am to 5 pm.

Website
https://www.rijksmuseum.nl/en
Rijksmuseum Map
https://goo.gl/maps/WjRNj11GzjM2

The Cheese Museum

One of the really popular museums in Amsterdam is the House of Anne Frank. People visit the place for its huge historical value.

However, right across the street from the famed Anne Frank House is another interesting place, though it is not as celebrated as the museum right in front of it.

You may not even notice the Cheese Museum since it looks like a regular café or snack bar. Nevertheless, this museum has been keeping alive a tradition that has been around for centuries. The cheese industry in Netherlands has about 600 years in its history. That history as well as the many different flavors of unique cheeses is preserved and highlighted in this museum.

So, who will be interested to visit such an odd museum? It's the food lovers, of course. Seeing row upon row of different cheeses with their own unique flavors is enough to make a foodie's heart leap twice. Of course, you can sample the different cheeses to your heart's content.

The Cheese Museum is located at Prinsensgracht 112, 1015 EA, Amsterdam. Admission is only one Euro. The place is open to visitors from 10 in the morning to 6 in the evening. The only downside to the place is that they don't have much space. That means they can't accommodate a large crowd of visitors.

Website

http://www.cheesemuseumamsterdam.com/

Cheese Museum Map

https://goo.gl/maps/fD5B78qdPo52

Van Gogh Museum

This is one of the more prestigious museums in the world. Mention the name Van Gogh and people almost instantly know who's being referred to. Obviously, the collection you'll find in this museum will be the works Vincent van Gogh. It also contains the works of other 19th century artists.

Another treasure trove in this museum is the collected letters of Van Gogh to his colleagues and family. They especially reveal his feelings toward his art and it gives us a window to look into the soul and inner workings of this one of a kind artist.

The museum is located within the Museum Quarter, so it won't be that hard to find. Its entrance is located at Paulus Potterstraat 7. The museum is usually open from 9 am to 6 pm. They also have different events scheduled every Friday.

Website

http://www.vangoghmuseum.nl/en

Van Gogh Museum Map

https://goo.gl/maps/HGFXW9ZTLwp

Stedelijk Museum

Stedelijk is the municipal museum of Amsterdam. It's dedicated to modern art – unlike the other collections you'll find elsewhere. It was established in the year 1895. It initially housed collections of different art works and historical items. It was only during the 1970's when this museum became dedicated to modern art.

The museum has undergone extensive renovation. Today it sports a more modern feel to it. Well, basically the design of the interior matches the type of collection it currently holds. Every now and then the museum also hosts lectures, concerts, films, and other performances, which is a treat in case you happen to be there for a special event.

The Stedelijk is open daily from 10 am to 6 pm. However, they open from 11 am to 10 pm on Thursdays. You'll find the entrance at Museumplein 10, Amsterdam.

Website

http://www.stedelijk.nl/en

Stedelijk Museum Map

https://goo.gl/maps/DKpXH1CJH3D2

Anne Frank House

The Anne Frank house is one of the really popular places to visit in Amsterdam. It's a solemn place that breathes the grim history of World War II. It literally attracts throngs of people; and unfortunately, you have to line up just to get a glimpse of the place where the Frank family and others hid from Nazi army.

The interior of the house is hollow and empty now. Yet in these quiet quarters lay the silent testimony of the people who lived there. Visitors will find actual items that belonged to the people who lived there. Anne Frank's original diary is on display along with her other notes. Some quotes from her writings are also on display.

The one hour tour will include a view of pretty much everything. A virtual tour will allow you to see the entire place. It will also provide visitors with a lot of background information. Note that the museum doesn't have facilities for people with disabilities. Remember, this is where people hid, so don't expect it to have wide open spaces.

Expect really long lines during summer. If you want to avoid the really long snaking lines of visitors from all over the world, then schedule your visit to the Anne Frank House from March to October. The museum is usually open from 9 am to 9 pm. The museum is located at Prinsengracht 267, 1016 GV, Amsterdam.

Website
http://www.annefrank.org/
Anne Frank House Map
https://goo.gl/maps/nv6Mej2YuHG2

The Museum of Prostitution
No visit to Amsterdam will be complete without a visit to one of the erotic museums there. The Museum of Prostitution is one of the best ones you will find. Now, this is one museum that isn't exactly child-

friendly. You should leave the kids at home if you're planning to visit this place. It's situated perfectly right in the middle of Amsterdam's red light district, in Binnenstad. It's pretty hard to miss. The tour of the place isn't going to last you an hour and the whole exhibition will cost you less than 10 euros.

You'll be treated to a short discourse on the history of prostitution in Amsterdam. It will also give you a first person point of view of what it's like to be behind the windows with the red lights. You'll learn first-hand what it feels like to be the girl sitting inside the glass casement, as it were.

An interesting part of the visit to this museum is the tour of the various chambers where the prostitutes perform their profession. The various implements and props will be explained to you and you'll have a lot of photo ops while you're in there. You can see it as a chance to be educated about the ins and outs of this one of a kind profession. Some people will come out displeased of course but there are those who will experience a small paradigm shift after the tour – how each person reacts is simply a subjective experience.

Website
http://www.redlightsecrets.com/
Museum of Prostitution Map
https://goo.gl/maps/XQNbVdED2V32

Science Center Nemo

This is one of the museums that will amaze young children. The place offers a lot of attractions that highlight the wonders of science while providing kids a lot of entertainment. Children can take part in many different experiments and understand just how the world works.

They'll have fun creating gigantic soap bubbles, figuring out how electronic gadgets work, and explore the mysteries of physics and chemistry. They'll learn the many characteristics of sound and visual media as well. The building itself is absolutely interesting – imagine walking into the very hull of a huge ship.

The Science Center Nemo is usually crowded from May to August, which is its peak season. The low season is from September to April. You'll find it on Oosterdok 2, 1011 VX Amsterdam. They're open from 10 am to 5:30 pm.

Website
https://www.nemosciencemuseum.nl/en/
Science Center Nemo Map
https://goo.gl/maps/AwiLQyE41NJ2

National Maritime Museum

The National Maritime Museum, or locally known as the Het Scheep-vaartmuseum, is also another interesting place for kids and adults. Much of the collections you'll find in this museum includes maritime artifacts – well, Amsterdam began as a fishing village and it was a center of trade with a natural port at one time in its history. Maritime travels and business is a big part of the history of the city.

There are exhibits that are specially tailored for kids such as Sal and Yori and Circus Sea, My Expo, and the Tale of the Whale.

The other exhibits are quite informational such as Navigational Instruments, Port 24/7, and See You in The Golden Age. There are sections of the museum where kids can play video games, view multimedia presentations, and other attractions that allow kids to learn and play.

The National Maritime Museum is open daily from 9 am to 5 pm. The museum will be closed on certain holidays. You can find the museum in Kattenburgerplein 1, 1018 KK Amsterdam.

Website
https://www.hetscheepvaartmuseum.nl/?t=English
National Maritime Museum Map
https://goo.gl/maps/PGjkQToczdR2

6

Best Art Galleries

The previous chapter enumerated some of the best museums that you can find in Amsterdam and in the Netherlands. Notice that a lot of these museums feature classic and contemporary artworks. Some of these important museums include the Stadsarchief (or the City Archive) which is full of Art Deco murals; Verzetsmuseum (the Museum of the Resistance) which features life in Amsterdam under Nazi Germany; Jewish Historical Museum which features Jewish art and the city's Jewish history; and the Hermitage Amsterdam that showcases collections that are on loan from the Hermitage Palace (St. Petersburg).

This book is focused on the short stay traveller, but I have included links and maps to the above-mentioned museums if you do have extra time to visit them.

Stadsarchief Website
https://www.amsterdam.nl/stadsarchief/english/home.en.html
Stadsarchief Map
https://goo.gl/maps/deHCDBZ3rhC2

Verzetsmuseum Website
https://www.verzetsmuseum.org/museum/en/museum
Verzetsmuseum Map
https://goo.gl/maps/tpA7o7XhPNL2

Jewish Historical Museum Website
http://www.jhm.nl/
Jewish Historical Museum Map
https://goo.gl/maps/Mgv25KNkrbE2

Hermitage Amsterdam Website
http://www.hermitage.nl/en/
Hermitage Amsterdam Map
https://goo.gl/maps/eDwPKUYh7q92

The following are some of the interesting art galleries in the city. Some of them take on a particular theme. There are plenty of these galleries where visitors can admire the art and also purchase some of the items that are on display.

Contemporary and Modern Art

If you're interested in taking home some of the best in contemporary art then just walk around the shopping district. You'll find a gallery in just about every block. For instance, the ArTicKs Gallery located on Singel 88 features the best in steel art. Their collections include works from different genres including punk, low brow, comic, stencil, and graffiti. The KochxBos Gallery on the other hand features the works of some of the brightest talents from various parts of the world. You'll find it on Anjeliersdwarsstraat 36.

ArTicKs Gallery Map
https://goo.gl/maps/wQnfSUHBmdE2
The KochxBos Gallery Map
https://goo.gl/maps/YJV881ybPhT2

Other galleries that feature modern and contemporary art include the Akinci Gallery in Lijnbaansgracht 317 1017 WZ Amsterdam; Arti et Amicitiae with an official address in Rokin 112, 1012 LB Amsterdam; and Bart, Galerie Amsterdam, which features the best and brightest of Amsterdam's artists. Bart is located in Bloemgracht 2, 1015TH Amsterdam.

Akinci Gallery Map
https://goo.gl/maps/bmtRgUMTsFp
Arti et Amicitiae Map
https://goo.gl/maps/bo1aeHqejyM2
Bart Galerie Amsterdam Map
https://goo.gl/maps/8YrKWNVsNcr

Now let's take a look at the galleries you should definitely visit in Amsterdam.

Torch Gallery

Established in 1984, Torch is one of the newer yet more popular art galleries in Amsterdam. It specializes in new media as well as photography. Much of the works on display take on a rather experimental theme. You can even say that the artists featured here take on rather bold strokes using new media as their paint brush. The gallery's current address is Lauriergracht 94, 1016 RN Amsterdam.

Website
http://www.torchgallery.com/
Torch Gallery Map
https://goo.gl/maps/d24Ce6rLb3s

Galerie Lieve Hemel

Galerie Lieve Hemel is the go to place for people who want to stick with purely realistic paintings. The collections mainly include works from Dutch artists. This art gallery is currently located at Nieuwe Spiegelstraat 3, 1017 DB Amsterdam having moved from its former address.

Website
http://www.lievehemel.nl/
Galerie Lieve Hemel
https://goo.gl/maps/MP5MYhn2xv52

Jaski Art Gallery

Have you ever heard of the CoBrA abstract movement? You'll find an extensive collection of art from that genre here in the Jaski Art Gallery. This gallery is the dream child of former tennis champion Tom Okker. The gallery's address is Nieuwe Spiegelstraat 29, 1017 DB Amsterdam.

Website
http://www.jaski.nl/home-2/
Jaski Art Gallery Map
https://goo.gl/maps/ze8rTVSEjRA2

Gerhard Hofland Gallery

Gerhard Hofland Gallery is one of the more ambitious galleries in Amsterdam. They feature some of the best artists in the Netherlands and Germany. The exhibits are often described as both striking and surprising. Needless to say, the artists and the gallery owner are striving hard to get museum recognition. The address of this art gallery is Bilderdijkstraat 165c, 1053 KP, Amsterdam.

Website
http://gerhardhofland.com/en/
Gerhard Hofland Gallery Map
https://goo.gl/maps/jRHQ48uZZnt

Carla Koch, Gallery

This gallery features the works of Carla Koch. The collection includes works that center on glass and ceramics as the primary medium. You'll find the gallery in Veemkade 500 (6th floor), building Detroit, 1019 HE Amsterdam.

Website
http://www.carlakoch.nl/
Carla Koch, Gallery Map
https://goo.gl/maps/2FWBrfdgkEo

Braggiotti Gallery

This art gallery mainly features glass art. It also highlights the best from local artists as well as works from artists from other countries. You'll find the gallery in Singel 424, 1016 AK Amsterdam.

Website
http://www.braggiotti.com/
Braggiotti Gallery Map
https://goo.gl/maps/wHpZMQb2pjt

7

A Potpourri of Flavors from Amsterdam's Restaurants

Amsterdam hasn't made its mark in the culinary world, yet. However, restaurants dot the city – and a good number of them have earned their very own Michelin stars. You'll find a mixture of culinary backgrounds and potpourri of different cuisines. It's definitely a place where good old homey Dutch cooking meets and greets the rest of the world. At times, you'll find a fusion as chefs, and everybody else manning the kitchen tries to outdo the other restaurant when coming up with something new.

The following is a short list of restaurants that serve the general public in Amsterdam. Note that some are pricier than others. The list also includes some interesting but not so popular restaurants.

Blue Spoon

Blue Spoon is the go-to place for the hungry guests who have booked rooms in the Andaz Hotel. They offer Dutch food with a bit of a French flair – or is it the other way around? Well anyway, it doesn't really matter because when the waiters walk by with a huge platter of food in hand, the flavorful aroma wafting in the air will be enough to make you forget which cuisine you're sampling.

If you're a fan of minimalist design, then the décor here won't disappoint. There is a touch of elegance in the simplicity of the ambiance in this place. You'll find Blue Spoon at Andaz Prinsengracht Hotel, Prinsengracht 587, 1016 HT. Meal prices here range from €40 to €45.

Website
http://hyatt.com/corporate/restaurants/Bluespoon/nl/Home/Con-tact.html
Blue Spoon Map
https://goo.gl/maps/FFJZfSczhkQ2

Mamouche

If you haven't tried Moroccan cuisine, then allow Mamouche to give you that well-deserved first taste. You can say that the flavors of the food here are slightly out of this world. Imagine the ingredients – oysters, scallops, tuna, orange dressing, figs, avocadoes, and goat's cheese.

The feel of the place is rather warm yet friendly. Diners also have the option to dine a la carte. Considering the neighborhood it's in (i.e.

De Pijp) expect young professionals to gather here at lunch time and after working hours. You'll find this restaurant at Quellijnstraat 104, 1072 XZ. Meal prices here average at €40.

Website
http://www.restaurantmamouche.nl/
Mamouche Map
https://goo.gl/maps/WL3hQrVXhsB2

Wink

Judging by the name of this restaurant, you can tell that it's playful and cheery. The red table tops actually add to that overall feel. It's a relatively small restaurant, and you may even be tempted to call it your mom's home kitchen. However, the chef working behind the scenes actually whip up miracles in their little hatch. It's one of those places where you can allow your taste buds to experience the very best of Dutch cooking mixed and matched with the best that pure talent can concoct.

You can find Wink at Govert Flinckstraat 326, 1073 CJ, which is easily accessible via Tram 4. They are open from Tuesdays to Saturdays from 6 in the evening to 10 pm. Food prices here average at 35 euros.

Website
http://www.bijwink.nl/
Wink Map
https://goo.gl/maps/JsQEfUxEci32

Serre

If formal dining is just too formal or if the food prices in fancy restaurants are just too high then you may want to tone things down a little at Serre. The place is definitely elegant, but it doesn't carry a lot of flair. You still get a great fine dining experience minus the crazy prices that may cut travel budget a bit short. Now, even though everything is scaled down at Serre, they still offer the classic Bibendum Menu, and the canal terrace provides an ecstatic view minus the usual rumble of city traffic you get from other places. This restaurant is at Hotel Okura, Ferdinand Bolstraat 333, 1072 LH. Meal prices average at 36 euros.

Website
https://www.okura.nl/nl/culinair/serre-restaurant/
Serre Map
https://goo.gl/maps/R8QkY9SPZ4H2

De Reiger

Care to dine in the old Amsterdam way? Then look for De Reiger since they offer pretty much that kind of dining experience. The menu here changes on a daily basis. Each day you'll be treated to a different set of flavors that only the Dutch can provide. The restaurant has preserved the ambiance of the good old days when that part of the city's quarter was reserved for the working class. The old prints are still up on the walls, and the deco lamps still bring back the feel of bygone decades.

Here's a quick tip – make sure to come early. Nevertheless, even though a line usually forms, the wait time isn't that long. You can find this restaurant at Nieuwe Leliestraat 34, 1015 ST. They are open from noon to 10:30 pm. Meal prices average at 38 euros.

Website
http://dereigeramsterdam.nl/#!/
De Reiger Map
https://goo.gl/maps/ntUDajW9b6B2

Wing Kee

If you're hungry for some Chinese food, then don't forget that wherever you go in the world, you will always find some sort of a China Town or a Chinese quarter. Now, not all Chinese food is the same, and some these restaurants have a certain specialties. Wing Kee is the sort of restaurant that serves really succulent food in generous servings.

You just have to try their roasted suckling pig – it's crispy and crackling. The meat is cooked to perfection – it's so tender it melts in your mouth. If you're not into eating a lot of pork, then you ought to at least try their roasted duck. Just like your traditional Chinese restaurant, you can find the roasted ducks hanging by the window, cooked golden brown succulently roasted.

Website

https://www.facebook.com/Wing-Kee-357051104343/

Wing Lee Map

https://goo.gl/maps/C2Vc5M3JfkC2

Japan Inn

Can't have enough of authentic Asian food? Then try the food from Japan Inn. The décor and mood of the place is rather modest. The tamed lighting matches the low key interiors quite nicely. Of course, they serve the best of Japanese cuisine. Of course, this is one of the places in the city Japanese expats and students find their way after a long day at work or school. You'll find Japan Inn at Leidsekruisstraat 4, 1017 RH. They're open from 5:30 pm to 11:30 pm. Meal prices here average at €22.

Website

http://www.japaninn.nl/

Japan Inn Map

https://goo.gl/maps/T9mGCgPphn22

Moeders

If you're in Amsterdam, then you ought to at least sample the authentic Dutch cuisine. If that's the type of flavor you want to get, then sample the food served in Moeders (translated as "mothers"). The walls of this restaurant are covered with pictures of mothers – the meals, of course, are cooked just the way Dutch moms would cook them.

If you want to sample all the food on the menu then order a sampler – it will have pretty much all the stuff you'll find on the menu. That way you get to sample the best of the local cuisine in one go. Moeders is located at Rozengracht 251, 1016 SX Amsterdam.

Website

http://www.moeders.com/en/home

Moeders Map

https://goo.gl/maps/nkydqUL35cp

Beddington's

In case you have the cash to burn, and you really want to try one of the best high-end restaurants in Amsterdam then try the food served in Beddington's. The restaurant has been around since 1983. The food served here is a fusion of Asian, English, and Dutch cuisine. You'll be treated to the best of Derbyshire home cooking with all the twists and turns to delight your taste buds. Meal prices here range from €48 to €55. They restaurant is open from Tuesdays to Saturdays from 7 pm onwards.

Website

https://www.facebook.com/Beddingtons-556445114402346/

Beddington's Map

https://goo.gl/maps/UNUXcgFYuNm

Restaurant Greetje

Restaurant Greetje takes Dutch cuisine and then takes it to a whole new level. Just try their stamppot; it tastes like the traditional dish but with a gleeful flavor added to it. The secret, of course, is to replace some of the ingredients to make a subtle twist in the flavor. The food is also plated to perfection. You can find this restaurant at Peperstraat 23-25. Meal prices start at €25. They're open from Sundays, and Tuesdays to Fridays from 6 to 10 in the evening. On Saturdays, they open from 6 to 11 in the evening.

Website

http://www.restaurantgreetje.nl/

Restaurant Greetje Map

https://goo.gl/maps/7TSYF1xEC4z

Razmataz

Razmataz is one of the few restaurants in Amsterdam that stays open from breakfast to dinner. The meals served here are mainly Mediterranean and French. Note that the menu changes with the season. The crowd that usually gathers here mainly includes the younger generation. They start coming in for a bit of morning coffee. In the evening, the guests stay a little longer for some after dinner drinks. You can find this restaurant at Hugo de Grootplein 7. Food prices here start at 20 euros. They're usually open from 8:30 am to 1 am. On some days, they open at 9 in the morning.

Website

http://www.razmataz.nl/#ramataz

Razmataz Map

https://goo.gl/maps/x47saFTdkW32

8

Shopping

Shopping in Amsterdam

Another thing that makes Amsterdam a popular tourist destination shopping. Visitors come here to shop for just about anything. Here you will find curious items, antiques, trinkets, strange souvenirs, and even diamonds. Shopping centers usually open at 9 in the morning and close at 6 in the evening. However, there are many late night shopping centers too, and they usually close at 9 pm.

The Shopping Neighborhoods

There are many streets and neighborhoods in Amsterdam that are lined with shops and boutiques. Close to the Central Station you'll immediately be greeted by a kilometer long shopping district from Nieuwedijk to Kalverstraat. There is no road traffic, so all you'll see are pedestrians, tourists, students, and other folks from different walks of life. The entire stretch of road is lined with shops and stalls displaying their wares.

If you're looking for gift items, bags, and other accessories then try the stores at Kalverstraat. They also have ice cream stores and restaurants in case you get hungry. On the same road, you'll also find the flower market. There you can find the world famous bulbs and tulips that you can take home with you. If you're looking for more signature items, then head out to the Oud Zuid district where you'll find shops with names like Gucci, Tommy Hilfiger, Cartier, and others.

Nieuwedijk Map
https://goo.gl/maps/wqTEiNgyvqH2
Kalverstraat Map
https://goo.gl/maps/djcjHv4iE5v
Kalverstraat Website
http://kalverstraat.amsterdam/en/shopsoverview
Oud Zuid District Map
https://goo.gl/maps/KnW5Uua14PQ2

Malls and Department Stores

Of course, there are also malls and department stores in the city. You'll find a lot of the imported stuff in these places. One of the most popular department stores is De Bijenkorf. If you want to see pretty much every mall in the city then walk on to the Dam square. The only mall that isn't on that square is Villa Arena.

De Bijenkorf Map
https://goo.gl/maps/AdcdZ6oscMx

Dam Square Map
https://goo.gl/maps/pHUyg6hSgD82

Let's take a lot at some of the best and unique stores in Amsterdam:

The American Book Center

This store has a very big variety of books of many different genres. The store has three floors and hosts a variety of events like book signings, meeting with authors and conferences. This store also has a wide variety of English magazines.

The store is open every day:

Monday, Tue, Wed, Fri, Sat: 10am – 8pm

Thurs: 10am – 9pm

Sun: 11am – 6pm

Website

http://www.abc.nl/

The American Book Center Map

https://goo.gl/maps/D8yuDvwkPb92

Iittala

The Dutch are famous for their love of design. The character of the Dutch design is minimalist, experimental and innovative. So these days the Dutch has fell in love with this store from Finland that is known for their excellent designs. This Finnish design brand specializes in design objects, tableware, and cookware.

Mon: 12:00pm – 6:00pm

Tue: Wed, Fri 10:00am – 6:00pm

Thu: 10:00am – 9:00pm

Sat: 10:00am – 6:00pm

Sun : 12:00pm – 6:00pm

Website

https://www.iittala.com/home

Map

https://goo.gl/maps/peRPKAX8gzr

HEMA

HEMA is a very popular chain of department stores all over the Netherlands.The interesting thing about HEMA is that they design and produce everything they sell.A Hema you will find almost anything you want, and you will have a unique Dutch shopping experience.

Mon – Wed:09:00am – 07:00pm

Thurs: 09:00am – 09:00pm

Fri – Sat: 09:00am –07:00pm

Sun: 12:00am – 06:00pm

Website

http://www.hemashop.com/

HEMA Map

https://goo.gl/maps/DWN21SQRJV22

Droog

Droog is probably one of the most interesting stores you will visit in Amsterdam.They are famous for cutting edge design and products.Droog uses unlikely or discarded materials and turns them into amazing products.

Tue – Sun 11:00am – 18:00pm

Mon –Closed

Website

http://www.droog.com/

Droog Map

https://goo.gl/maps/SzsKixuBHzr

If you're interested in shopping for antiques, then your best shot is to look for antique shops in the city's shopping market. There you'll find food, clothing items, some fixtures, and antiques. The markets are only a short walk away from the city center.

I have made a list of the top markets and vintage stores:

De Looier Arts & Antiques

This place might not look it from the outside, but its the largest and most popular antique market in the Netherlands. You can find almost anything in this big treasure chest. This store has anything from old watches to old paintings. This is one of my favorite markets in Amsterdam, and you will leave with something special.

-Elandsgracht 109, 1016 TT Amsterdam

The store is not open every day:

Mon,Wed,Thu,Fi : 10am - 6pm

Tue: Closed

Sat ,Sun :10am - 5pm

De Looier Arts & Antiques Map

https://goo.gl/maps/Yf4XXcTP1zA2

Wini Vintage

If you are into vintage clothing, then look no further than Wini. You will find good quality vintage clothing and at a reasonable price. The main focus in this store is for women, but they have a small collection of vintage men's clothing.

-Haarlemmerstraat 29, 1013 EJ Amsterdam

Wini is Open every day:

Mon - Wed: 10:30am - 6:00pm

Thurs 10:30am - 6.30pm

Fri and Sat: 10:30am - 6:00pm

Sun: 12.00pm - 6:00pm

Website

http://winivintage.nl/

Wini Vintage Map

https://goo.gl/maps/HG3aiJsMA752

Waterlooplein Markt

Waterlooplein is the most popular flea market in Amsterdam and many tourist flocks here to get to the best goods first. This is a great place to find a bargain and negotiate a good price.Stand your ground with some of the pushy sellers and make sure you get a reasonable price.On Saturdays, the market turns into organic farmers heaven.

-Waterlooplein 2, Amsterdam

Mon - Fri: 09:00am - 05:30pm

Sat: 8:30am - 5:30pm

Website

http://www.waterloopleinmarkt.nl/

Waterlooplein Markt Map

https://goo.gl/maps/sD5bEVxPQn72

Noordermarkt

This amazing open-air market is a great place to visit if you like great food and vintage goods.The combination of the two is awesome and its a great to shop while snacking on some Dutch cheese.All the organic farmers in the Netherlands bring their goods to be sold hear.If you are in Amsterdam on a Monday, then drop into Noordermarkt because they market will sell a wide variety of antique goods, ranging from clothes to books.

Opening Times:

Mon: 9:00am – 2:00pm

Sat 9:00am – 4:00pm

Website

http://www.noordermarkt-amsterdam.nl/

Noordermarkt Map

https://goo.gl/maps/LeJJgnvkqmL2

9

Cafe's (coffee)

When you're in Amsterdam, you should remember that there is a difference between a café and a coffee shop. A café is where you get your coffee and snacks, but a coffee shop is something else. Yes, it's one of those places where you can legally smoke marijuana, and other kinds of soft drugs. We'll deal with those places later in this book.

For now, you'll find some of the best places to get your coffee in the list below:

Café Het Paleis

This café is conveniently located near Dam square, where many of the tourist sites and places of interest are located. It's a great place to take a break, have a beer or a cup of coffee along with some pastries before heading out to your next destination. Try their apple tarts and sandwiches. You'll find it at Paleisstraat 16.

Website
https://www.facebook.com/cafehetpaleis
Café Het Paleis Map
https://goo.gl/maps/5NyP4cNgktw

Pannenkoekenhuis Upstairs

Aside from the coffee, Pannenkoekenhuis serves some of the best treats to help you get through a hangover. Their Dutch pancakes are their signature treats. The food is a bit pricey but the location is great – nothing like fresh air to set things straight. You'll find this café at Grimburgwal 2.

Website
http://www.upstairspannenkoeken.nl/
Pannenkoekenhuis Upstairs Map
https://goo.gl/maps/tUUJE1pMP4n

Poco Loco

You can come to Poco Loco for your morning coffee to start your day. You can also return to the place to cap off your night with some of the best local beer. You should also try their tapas just to go with your drinks. Expect this café to be a bit crowded – it's that popular. You'll find it at Nieuwmarkt 24.

Website
https://www.facebook.com/CafePocoLoco
Poco Loco Map
https://goo.gl/maps/1NbCXkhyDiy

Singel 404

You should avoid this café during lunch time. It is usually packed with students lining up for a meal. Well, sometimes they bring more tables out, which gives you a good view of the canal but even then, if you come in late you may have to wait a while to get a seat. Afternoons here are less crowded. They even serve a good brew of coffee with some cake to match your mood.

Website

https://www.facebook.com/Lunchcafe-Singel-404-476001639099605/

Singel 404 Map

https://goo.gl/maps/B9ZBrxTddyz

10

Bars and Clubs

Amsterdam has an awesome nightlife, and you will find great places to have fun if you have a lot of time to explore the city.The problem is you probably won't have the time to walk around Amsterdam hoping you find the right place.So I made a list of the best bars and clubs for you to consider.

The Tara

The Tara use to be an English Pub, but these days its has a real Amsterdam flavour mixed with the concepts of a traditional British pub.It is modern, cosy, and the food is good.If you are looking for good beer in a warm and cosy atmosphere, then visit the Tara.The Tara shows popular sports events and has live music on some evenings.The Tara has three bars, seven rooms and two sidewalk terraces.

Opening Times: Monday to Sunday 10 am - 1 am
Website
http://thetara.com/
The Tara Map
https://goo.gl/maps/LPpM17ygedu

Brouwerij 't IJ

This is a special location in Amsterdam.Firstly it's located in an old Windmill, and secondly it's one of the best microbreweries in the city.This bar has an amazing collection of high-quality beers.If you visit one bar in Amsterdam, then visit the Brouwerij IJ.

Open Daily from 2 pm – 8 pm

Website

http://www.brouwerijhetij.nl/

Brouwerij 't IJ Map

https://goo.gl/maps/mugmjkP8TLT2

Hanneke's Boom

This place looks more like an old beach house than a bar and it's built right next to water.Hanneke's Boom is one of the most popular hangouts in Amsterdam and is built and decorated with second-hand items.In the summer, the locals visit the bar by boat and it gets crowded.Great spot for a cold beer in the summer.This place is over 300 years old so visit this unique spot.Come by boat or on foot.

Website

http://www.hannekesboom.nl/en/

Hanneke's Boom Map

https://goo.gl/maps/qRvYDSe1VDQ2

Whiskycafé L&B

Whiskycafé L&B stock around 1400 different types of Whisky and Bourbon from around the world.The staff at this bar are very knowledgeable about whisky, so you will easily be pointed in the right direction if the large selection becomes overwhelming.This bar is very relaxed but has a nice and warm atmosphere.

Opening Times:

Sun – Thurs 8 pm – 3 am

Fri – Sat 8pm – 4 am

Website

http://www.whiskyproeverijen.nl/cafe.htm

Whiskycafé L&B Map

https://goo.gl/maps/xXiiWLZPBrt

De Zotte

Belgian beer lovers usually find their way to De Zotte. You can find several good brews here for you to sample. Don't forget to get either grilled lamb or steak to go with your drink. You'll find this bar and café at Raamstraat 29.

Opening times:

Mon – Thurs 4pm –1am

Fri – Sat 2pm – 3am

Website

https://www.facebook.com/sosdezotte

De Zotte Map

https://goo.gl/maps/hBfNggZar8K2

Van Kerkwijk

At first glance, you might think that this café is nothing more than shady back alley beer pub south of the Dam square. Well, that's what you'll get when you look at the place from the outside. Walk in and you'll find it buzzing with life. This café is quite popular with its rather rustic menu. Most of the meals have a rather French twist but the steaks are godly well-seasoned – something that will make you come back again and again. You'll find the place at Nes 41.

Opening Times:

Open Daily from 11am – 1am

Website

http://www.caferestaurantvankerkwijk.nl/

Van Kerkwijk Map

https://goo.gl/maps/3EUqthqqPns

Getto

Getto is the place where you can get great cocktails and great burgers. Each burger on the menu is named after a drag queen that performs there. Check out their website to find out who is performing. You'll find this one of a kind bar and café at Warmoesstraat.

Opening Times:
Sun 4:30pm: – 12:00am
Tues , Wed , Thurs 4:30pm –1:00am
Fri 4:30pm – 2:00am
Website
http://www.getto.nl/
Getto Map
https://goo.gl/maps/AtwaFLrs5RK2

Studio 80

Although this is kind of a hipster hangout, it is a one of the best clubs in Amsterdam.The DJ's at the club are great, and they focus on a type of minimal techno music.This is one of the trendiest clubs in Amsterdam, and you should expect to see the weird and wonderful of Amsterdam making their appearance.So if you have an open mind then visit Studio 80.
Website
http://www.studio-80.nl/
Studio 80 Map
https://goo.gl/maps/Mrd4SJsWT4H2

Bitterzoet

If you are not into techno and you are looking for something more laid back, then this is the club for you.A good way to describe Bitterroot's sound is that it's a mix between urban, jazz and soul.This club has a dark and sexy feeling to it.Friday's in Bitterzoet is funk and soul night, so if that's your thing then pop into the club.
Website
https://www.bitterzoet.com/#/home
Bitterzoet Map
https://goo.gl/maps/V8wTod3EYE62

Sugar Factory

Sugar Factory is one of the unique clubs in Amsterdam where performance and clubbing meet and creates something you will only find in Amsterdam.The club used to be a theatre, and a large stage is right next to the dance floor where a variety of performance clubbing happens while the club is in full steam.Think of Sugar Factory as a Dynamic playground for the open-minded.

Website
https://www.sugarfactory.nl/lang/en/
Sugar Factory Map
https://goo.gl/maps/XQBzp8WLjH72

Jimmy Woo

This is the place to be seen in Amsterdam.If you want to be surrounded by Dutch Supermodels and Celebrities, then go to Jimmy Woo.The club has a dark smokey atmosphere and plays a mix of Hip Hop and House Music.

Website
https://www.facebook.com/JimmyWooLounge
Jimmy Woo Map
https://goo.gl/maps/8RdDio4FQGz

11

Only in Amsterdam

Only in Amsterdam

Each place on earth has something unique to offer. Just like many of the popular touristy places in the world, Amsterdam has many unique offerings. In this chapter you'll find some of the things that you can only find in this city.

Coffee Shops

There's no better way to say it than just to be candid about it and just say it. One of the reasons why some people visit Amsterdam is to try the coffee shops. Coffee shops in this city, as you know, are not little snack bars that serve nice smelling hot coffee. It's a place where they sell soft drugs, marijuana, and cannabis.

Mentioning that in this book doesn't mean that the author condones or promotes the use of controlled substances. Nevertheless, these shops are unique to Amsterdam and spending some time smoking pot here is one of the truly unique things that people can do when they visit the city.

I made a list of the best coffee shops in Amsterdam for those of you considering to visit a coffee shop.

Barney's Coffeeshop

What makes this place special? Well, it's located in a 500-year-old building. This shops has won a few high times awards and serves great food.

Open Daily from 7am - 10pm

-Haarlemmerstraat 102, 1013 EW Amsterdam

Website

https://barneys.biz/

Barney's Coffeeshop Map

https://goo.gl/maps/27pU3EY2RJ62

Bluebird

Bluebird was founded in 1982 and is nearby the red light district. The food at Bluebird is excellent, and the staff speaks English well.

Open Daily from 9 am - 1:30 am

-Sint Antoniesbreestraat 71, 1011 HB Amsterdam

Bluebird Map

https://goo.gl/maps/eANWrXxJL2p

The Bulldog

Everybody in Amsterdam knows about the Bulldog.If you think about Amsterdam Coffee Shops, then you think the Bulldog.The Bulldog was the first coffee shop in Amsterdam, and the original Bulldog is located in a former Amsterdam Police Station.There are now a few new Bulldog shops around, but I recommend you visit the original shop in Leidseplein 15.

The Bulldog is open daily from 10am-1am

-Leidseplein 15, 1017 PS Amsterdam

Website

http://www.thebulldog.com/

The Bulldog Map

https://goo.gl/maps/s3MNdr38sKu

Smoke Palace

If you want to have a coffee shop experience away from the crowds in a very relaxed setting, then visit Smoke Palace.Smoke Place is located in the eastern district of Amsterdam.

Open Daily from 9 am -1 am

-Linnaeusstraat 83 HS, 1093 EK Amsterdam

Website

http://www.smokepalace.nl/

Smoke Palace Map

https://goo.gl/maps/cwmGfgzo6J92

Smart Shops

Smart shops in Amsterdam are pretty much the same as coffee shops - with a slight difference of course. Smart shops, just like coffee shops, sell soft drugs, but they only sell smart drugs (i.e. the ones that stimulate the brain to improve memory and cognitive functions).

You can imagine students flocking here whenever there are exams. Here you'll find herbal medicines that are touted to improve your brain's functions. Herbal products like magic mushrooms, Gingko Biloba, Cola nut, and Guarana among others.The first smart shop in Amsterdam was Kokopelli.

Kokopelli.

This is one of the 10 Smart Shops left in Amsterdam and it was also the first.They were the trendsetters with selling magic mushrooms after they started their business with energy drinks and herbs.

-Warmoesstraat 12, 1012 JD Amsterdam

Website

http://www.kokopelli.nl/head

Kokopelli Map

https://goo.gl/maps/qs2j7Cev3pH2

Smart Shops Map

https://goo.gl/maps/SyEMSksr7H82

RED LIGHT DISTRICT

Amsterdam's Red Light District is another popular destination for many tourists. As you should know, prostitution is a legal profession in this city. Visitors have different reactions. Some come here with a sense of excitement, some look at the red fringed windows and stare in shock, while others giggle in a celebratory fashion. Now and then you will find busloads of tourists from different countries toting their beloved cameras – however, do take note that it is illegal to take pictures of the female entertainers. You'll find yourself and your camera in the wrong side of the law after that.

There are Red Light District tours if you are interested. You'll get lots of information about the place and one of the oldest industries in the world. Believe it or not, the RLD is actually one of the safest parts of Amsterdam. Security is pretty high with a lot of policemen on site. If you're planning to visit one of the brothels, peep shows, porno shows, and sex shops, you won't have to worry about getting robbed. Nevertheless, you should watch out for pickpockets since the streets tend to be quite crowded.

Red Light District Map

https://goo.gl/maps/KJ6xRCZL9Wq

The Amsterdam Theaters Scene

Now, there's really more to Amsterdam than just drugs and sex. It's actually rich in history and culture. In fact, the place has a lively theater scene. Walk along Nes street stroll around the Leidseplein you'll find some of the best theaters in the city. Some of the performances are quite notable.

Website

http://www.theateramsterdam.nl/en/

Amsterdam and Art

They have the Van Gogh Museum and a plethora of other museums and art galleries that dot the city. Isn't that enough to convince you that art is a huge part of Dutch life and culture? Check out the addresses of the different art galleries and museums in the other chapters of this book.

Life in the Open Road

Bicycles are a staple in the lives of the people of Amsterdam. You can't say that you have truly mingled with the locals until you have tried their wheels. The bicycle scene gets even more interesting at night when the city lights come alive, and the many bridges get lighted. Start biking at Leidseplein and watch the city come alive as you get to Kerkstraat and the rest of Amsterdam.

Bicycle Website
http://www.rent-a-bike-amsterdam.com/?lang=en
Bicycle Rental Map
https://goo.gl/maps/4LL4wfQPUY32

12

Sample 3 Day Itinerary

You can create your own 3 day itineraries given the places mentioned in this book. Of course, you will still need to work out some of the details like room and board reservations and transportation costs. You should buy a

Now, here's a sample three-day itinerary so you can have an idea how to set things up.

Day 1

9 am – 9 am – Rijksmuseum. Expect the place to be a bit crowded.

Tip: Get a map of the museum – it's pretty big. Spend three hours here.

Noon: Lunch time. Go to Go to Vondelpark and have lunch at Blauwe Theehuis. You'll stay here for about an hour or two.

2 pm – Van Gogh Museum

Tip: Get your ticket online and you can avoid the long queue of people by taking the priority line. The tour will take 2 to 3 hours.

5 pm – Museumplein – here you can watch the people play sports or better yet you can join in on the fun. It's a great place to meet the locals. You're stay here will take less than an hour.

6 pm –Canal Dinner Cruise – You will have dinner while on a boat cruise touring the city. The tour will last 3 hours and that will include dinner.

Day 2

9 am – Anne Frank House – take the tour, which will last about an hour or two.

11 am – Cheese Museum – Look around and enjoy the sight of many cheeses. You may even sample some of the cheeses if you like. The visit will last less than an hour.

Noon – Have lunch at the Jordaan – Take your pick and choose any of the many restaurants here. If you're not particularly hungry then grab a snack in one of the bars.

2 pm – Flower Market – Going to the flower market will be a bit of a stretch if you're on a bike. Nevertheless, the trip is worth it once you're at the flower market. You'll stay here for an hour.

Tip: If you want to take flowers home with you as souvenirs make sure to check the health inspection certificate of the flower packs before you buy them. The certification will tell you if the flower variant you're buying can be brought overseas.

3 pm – Go shopping – since you're already near

6 pm – Red Light District – roam around the Red Light District and enjoy the view. Try the services of the different shops if you want. There are bars and restaurants here where you can have your dinner.

Day 3

9 am – Science Center Nemo – this is a great place to bring the children along. Stay here for 1 to 3 hours

Noon – Lunch in Leiden Square at a restaurant of your choice. Stay here for 1 to 2 hours

2 pm –Albert Cuyp Market – Make sure to sample the Stroopwafels. Enjoy the frenzy of the market scene and look for a trinket that you can bring home with you. You may even find a piece of art that will inspire you. Shop here for 2 hours.

4 or 5 pm – Heineken – your Dutch experience won't be complete if you don't sample their beers and Heineken is the best place to get the best Dutch beer.

6 pm – Concertgebouw – enjoy the music at a live concert or watch a show in a theater if there is one. Make sure to try that distinct Dutch cultural experience while you're there.

8 pm – Bar hopping – it's your last night, better try some of the concoctions from one or two local bars.

13

Conclusion

I want to thank you for reading this book!I sincerely hope that you received value from it!